What Do Illustrators Do?

What Do Illustrators Do?

Written and Illustrated by

Eileen Christelow

CLARION BOOKS/New York

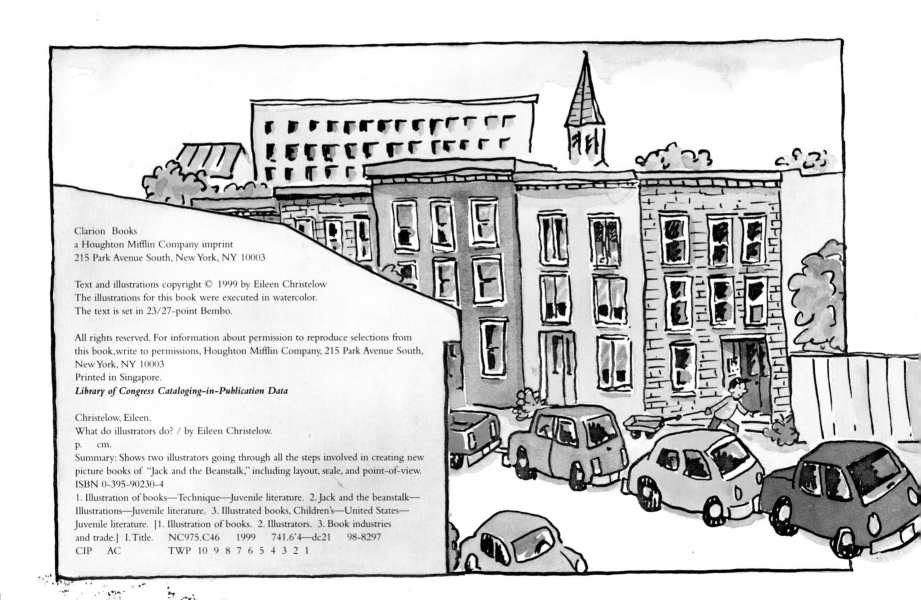

Clarion Books
a Houghton Mifflin Company imprint
215 Park Avenue South, New York, NY 10003

Text and illustrations copyright © 1999 by Eileen Christelow
The illustrations for this book were executed in watercolor.
The text is set in 23/27-point Bembo.

Printed in Singapore.
Library of Congress Cataloging-in-Publication Data

Christelow, Eileen.
What do illustrators do? / by Eileen Christelow.
p.   cm.
Summary: Shows two illustrators going through all the steps involved in creating new
picture books of "Jack and the Beanstalk," including layout, scale, and point-of-view.
ISBN 0-395-90230-4
1. Illustration of books—Technique—Juvenile literature. 2. Jack and the beanstalk—
Illustrations—Juvenile literature. 3. Illustrated books, Children's—United States—
Juvenile literature. [1. Illustration of books. 2. Illustrators. 3. Book industries
and trade.] I. Title.   NC975.C46   1999   741.6'4—dc21   98-8297
CIP   AC   TWP 10 9 8 7 6 5 4 3 2 1

W hat do illustrators do?
They tell stories with pictures.
This picture shows where
two illustrators live and work.

5

Suppose those two illustrators each
decided to illustrate *Jack and the Beanstalk.*
Would they tell the story the same way?
Would they draw the same kind of pictures?

First, illustrators decide which scenes
in the story they want to illustrate . . .

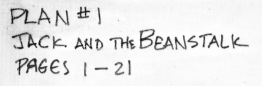

PLAN #1
JACK AND THE BEANSTALK
PAGES 1 — 21

half title page ①

dedication ② Title page ③

④ Story starts here ⑤

⑥ the beanstalk! ⑦

⑧ climbs the beanstalk ⑨

⑩ the top → a castle ⑪

⑫ "I'll knock on the door" "Oh no!" ⑬

⑭ "Help!" ⑮

⑯ "Fee Fie..." the hen ⑰

⑱ Giant sleeps   Jack escapes ⑲

⑳ The happy hen lays eggs of gold ㉑

A plan shows which pictures go on which pages.

I don't remember this story. Maybe Leonard does.

9

The Story of
JACK and the
BEANSTALK

It's about a boy who plants a magic bean.

The bean sprouts and it grows and GROWS right through the clouds!

Jack climbs to the top of the beanstalk.

What's up there?

A mean, wicked GIANT!

YIKES!

Don't worry! Jack hides. Then, when the giant is asleep, Jack steals the hen that lays golden eggs.

He steals?

The hen wants to be stolen! She hates living with the giant!

So Jack rescues the hen . . . .

Does he become rich and live happily ever after?

He does, but then he climbs the beanstalk two more times.

He takes a sack of gold coins and then a singing harp while the giant is asleep.

But the harp sings and the giant wakes up! He chases Jack . . . .

After illustrators make a plan for their book, they need to make a **dummy**. (A dummy is a model of the book.) First they decide what shape and size the book will be.

Then they make **sketches** of the pictures that will go on each page of the dummy.

The first sketches are often rough scribbles on tracing paper.

This is how we look when we are rough sketches.

As they are sketching, illustrators need to decide how things will look: the characters, their clothes, the setting.

Illustrators can use their imaginations or they may have to do some research.

Some illustrators are also authors. They can change their story as they work on the sketches.

Each illustration has
a different problem.
For instance: From what
point of view do you draw
the magic bean being planted?

How do you draw a beanstalk
so it looks like it's growing?

There is usually more than one way to solve the same problem.

Wow, Mom! The beanstalk must be enormous. Look at the roots!

That night, on the roof directly over Jacqueline's bedroom, the magic bean started to grow. It grew and grew and grew.....

Those roots are huge compared to Jacqueline!

Here is another problem:
How do you make a beanstalk
look really TALL?

Illustrators need to think about the design of each page.

Oops! If the giant doesn't look BIG enough or SCARY enough, the illustrator will draw that picture again.

...and what would Jack see when he looks up at the giant?

These pictures are scarier! And we can only see part of the giant.

Which picture do you think he should use in the book?

23

How would it feel
to run across a table
right under the nose
of a sleeping GIANT?

Illustrators need to draw
how their characters feel.
(Sometimes they make
faces in a mirror to see how
an expression would look.)

Raised eyebrows?
Eyes wide open?
Mouth open?

Jacqueline tiptoed across the table.
"Hurry up!" whispered the hen. "She
never sleeps for long!"

Sometimes illustrators
need someone else
to model for them.

Each illustrator has a different **style** of drawing, just as every person has a different style of handwriting.

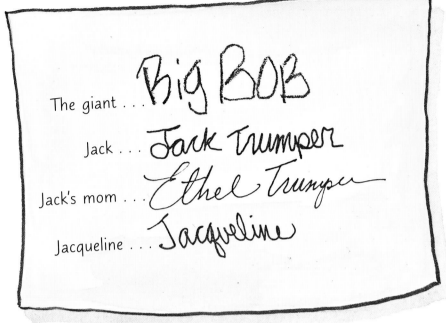

The giant . . . Big Bob

Jack . . . Jack Trumper

Jack's mom . . . Ethel Trumper

Jacqueline . . . Jacqueline

Different styles for drawing Jack and Jacqueline

We're trying a new style.

27

When illustrators have finished
their dummies, they show them
to the editor and the designer at the
publishing company.

The editor decides whether the
pictures tell the story.

The designer makes suggestions about the design of the book.

She chooses the typeface for the words and the cover.

Sample typefaces for title:

Jack and the Beanstalk

Jack and the Beanstalk

Jack and the Beanstalk

Sample typefaces for text:

(easy to read)

While Jacqueline slept in her bedroom below, the magic bean grew . . . and grew . . .

(not so easy to read)

While Jacqueline slept in her bedroom below, the magic bean grew . . . and grew . . .

Illustrators need to decide how they want to do the finished illustrations. They can draw different kinds of lines and textures with different kinds of tools.

pencil

pen with flexible point

brush

felt tip pen

They can color their illustrations with paint, pastels, pencils, or crayons...

I'm experimenting. I've tried watercolors, watercolor crayons, and colored pencils.

watercolors

watercolor crayons

colored pencils

31

They can do an illustration without any black line at all!

Illustrators need to choose the paper they want to use for their finished illustrations.

Some papers are good for watercolor, others for pastel, others for pencil... Some are smooth. Some are textured.

Illustrators go to art stores to buy their supplies.

Illustrators often use a lightbox to trace their drawings onto their new paper.

Sometimes illustrators
throw away their pictures
and start again.

Sometimes they change the colors.

Too many cool colors! Blue flowers, blue shoes, green leaves.

Cool colors make you feel cool, calm, relaxed or sometimes sad.

I need to add some warm colors - reds, oranges, yellows.

Warm colors make you feel bright, wild, loud, red hot!

Well, maybe not that many!

Or they may change the composition.

 This picture is confusing! It's hard to see what's happening.

 Should I put Jack in front of the giant? Should the giant lean to the left?

 The composition of this page would be better if we _both_ sit in this corner!

It can take months to finish all the illustrations for a picture book.

Before they are sent to the publisher, they need to be checked to make sure nothing is left out.

At last! I've finished all 32 pages and the cover!

It looks great Mom.

Except here. You forgot the polka dots on Jacqueline's shirt.

Oh phooey!

She also forgot to feed me this morning!

Don't worry! Once they finish the books, they'll pay attention to us again.

He's working on the cover...

I'm finished!

Me too! Can I see your book?

Illustrators often do the cover of the book last. The cover tells a lot about a story: What is it about? Does it look interesting?

The cover is a clue to how the illustrator will tell the story. Would these covers make you want to read the books?

This illustration tells how the two illustrators celebrated when they finally finished all that work!